The Art of the Northwest Coast Indians

Thunderbird and Whale,
Kwakiutl, painted wood,
Peabody Museum,
Harvard University,
photograph by Alfred Tamarin

by SHIRLEY GLUBOK

Designed by Gerard Nook

Macmillan Publishing Co., Inc.
New York
Collier Macmillan Publishers
London

The author gratefully acknowledges the assistance of:
Richard Conn, Curator of Native Arts, The Denver Art Museum;
Sara Stockover and *Michael Pope*

Other books by Shirley Glubok:

THE ART OF ANCIENT EGYPT
THE ART OF LANDS IN THE BIBLE
THE ART OF ANCIENT GREECE
THE ART OF THE NORTH AMERICAN INDIAN
THE ART OF THE ESKIMO
THE ART OF ANCIENT ROME
THE ART OF AFRICA
ART AND ARCHAEOLOGY
THE ART OF ANCIENT PERU
THE ART OF THE ETRUSCANS
THE ART OF ANCIENT MEXICO
KNIGHTS IN ARMOR
THE ART OF INDIA
THE ART OF JAPAN
THE ART OF COLONIAL AMERICA
THE ART OF THE SOUTHWEST INDIANS
THE ART OF THE OLD WEST
THE ART OF THE NEW AMERICAN NATION
THE ART OF THE SPANISH IN THE UNITED STATES AND PUERTO RICO
THE ART OF CHINA
THE ART OF AMERICA FROM JACKSON TO LINCOLN
THE ART OF AMERICA IN THE GILDED AGE
THE ART OF AMERICA IN THE EARLY TWENTIETH CENTURY
THE FALL OF THE AZTECS
THE FALL OF THE INCAS
DISCOVERING TUT-ANKH-AMEN'S TOMB
DISCOVERING THE ROYAL TOMBS AT UR
DIGGING IN ASSYRIA
HOME AND CHILD LIFE IN COLONIAL DAYS

Front cover illustration: Headdress frontlet, Tlingit, painted wood
with shell inlay, The Brooklyn Museum, Gift of Princess Gourielli.
Back cover illustration: Basket, Tlingit, spruce root and bear grass,
Fred Harvey Fine Arts Collection, The Heard Museum, Phoenix, Arizona,
photograph by Alfred Tamarin.

Macmillan Publishing Co., Inc., 866 Third Avenue, New York, N.Y. 10022
Collier-Macmillan Canada Ltd.
Printed in the United States of America

1 2 3 4 5 6 7 8 9 10

Library of Congress Cataloging in Publication Data
Glubok, Shirley. The art of the Northwest Coast Indians.
1. Indians of North America—Northwest coast of North America—
Art—Juvenile literature. [1. Indians of North America—
Northwest coast of North America—Art] I. Nook, Gerard, ill. II. Title.
E78.N78G58 709'.01'1 74-22384 ISBN 0-02-736150-0

Mechanical headdress, Kwakiutl,
painted wood and muslin,
Museum of the American Indian,
Heye Foundation

Along the Pacific Ocean from the mouth of the Columbia River in northern Oregon to Yakutat Bay in southern Alaska, the seacoast is broken by bays and inlets and dotted with hundreds of islands. On these islands and on the narrow strip of land between the ocean and the high mountains to the east live groups of Indian people. Among them are the Kwakiutl, Tlingit, Nootka, Tsimshian, Haida and Bella Coola. They speak different languages and have different customs, yet these groups are alike in many of their ways.

The first Europeans to see the Northwest Coast were Russian explorers who landed there in 1741. Then a Spanish ship arrived in 1774. An English captain, James Cook, on his third voyage of exploration in 1778, spent some time in the area. He collected sea otter furs which were taken to China, where they were highly prized. Soon afterward both European and American ships came to trade for the valuable animal skins. White settlers followed, around the middle of the nineteenth century, and their influence began to change the lives of the Indians. Yet many of the old practices remained and still continue today.

Photograph by
Edward S. Curtis, 1914

The Indians of the Northwest Coast usually built their villages along sheltered beaches near rivers that would supply fresh water. The houses, made of long planks of wood laid over a framework of logs, were built in a single row.

Each house was occupied by several families that were related. They sat, slept and stored their possessions on high platforms built along the walls and prepared their meals over open fires. In front of the houses stood totem poles, tall columns of cedar wood that were carved and painted with family emblems and figures relating to legends about the history of the family.

Among the Northwest Coast Indians every person is born into a clan, or group of families with the same ancestors. This system of relationships is still important today. The related families share legends about their clan's history and its descent from supernatural beings, animals and birds, as well as people. Representations of these characters, who are thought of as guardians, are called totems or crests.

The carved posts at left represent an eagle, which was the totem that the owner inherited from his father's side of the family, and a grizzly bear, the totem of his mother's side. At right is a post that supported roof beams inside a large house. House posts were the earliest type of totem pole. Both of these photographs were taken in Kwakiutl villages in Alaska in the early twentieth century. Almost no Northwest Coast art exists today that was created before the eighteenth century, because the materials used by the Indians are perishable in the damp climate of the area.

Photograph by
Edward S. Curtis, 1914

Totem poles were often used as doorways, with openings for entry, or as memorials to a dead leader. Some were as much as seventy feet tall. They were symbols of family pride and wealth. Totem poles were carved from great cedar logs while in a horizontal position. Starting from the top, the design was outlined

Totem poles at Kitwanga, British Columbia, Canadian National Railways

Photograph by
E. H. Harriman, 1899.
Library of Congress

with chalk, then carved out roughly with an ax. Smaller tools were used to carve away the background to bring out the design. Then the totem pole was painted. Brushes were made of animal hair or porcupine quills set in a wooden handle. Black paint was made from charcoal or soot; red and yellow came from ocher, an earth containing iron, and white from lime made by burning clam shells. After commercial paints were brought to the area in the 1880's, ordinary house paint was used.

The fronts of houses were often painted with totem figures. The painting on the Tlingit house above is typical of Northwest Coast designs, which often show two profiles, or side views, of an animal's body at the same time, as if the animal had been split down the middle from its neck to its tail, spread apart and flattened out. It also shows parts of the animal's skeleton and internal organs.

Denver Art Museum, photograph by Alfred Tamarin

The brown bear is an important totem among the Tlingit. A story is told of a youth who was captured by a female bear and was forced to marry her. He finally escaped from his animal wife, then took the bear as his family crest.

A brown bear seated like a human was carved and painted on a large wooden screen in the house of Chief Shakes in Alaska. The hole between the bear's outspread legs was used as a doorway. Smaller seated bears fill the spaces on the ears, and faces are painted on the eyes and nose. On the hands, elbows and knees are eye forms representing joints. Northwest Coast Indian artists fill in every possible space with designs.

The panel at right is painted with a scene from a legend about Killer Whale

American Museum of Natural History

being carried away by Lightning Snake, Wolf and Thunderbird, a powerful mythical figure. Thunderbird could cause storms and lightning by flapping his tremendous wings. This panel stood at the back of a Nootka house on Vancouver Island, British Columbia. It is made of thin boards cut from a red cedar tree; roots from this tree join the boards together. Oil from salmon eggs that were mashed by chewing them was mixed with pigments, or colors, for the paints.

Both of these screens were made around the middle of the nineteenth century, which is considered the most important period in Northwest Coast Indian art.

Photograph by C. F. Newcombe, 1913,
British Columbia Provincial Museum, Victoria

A screen carved and painted with the crest of a Tsimshian clan was photographed in front of a house in British Columbia, above.

During their winter ceremonies the Kwakiutl hung large painted cotton cloths on house walls. The man standing in front of the painted cloth at right is dressed for a ceremony. At his feet is a large feast dish. The painting on the cloth tells about Raven, a supernatural being who could transform himself into anything at any time. According to legend, there was a time when the world was in darkness. The sun, moon and stars were kept in three wooden boxes by a powerful magician. Raven transformed himself into the magician's grandchild, stole the boxes and set the sun free to give the people light. It went up in the sky in a blazing roar. The frightened people ran in all directions. The ones wearing bird or animal skins became those creatures. The ones wearing nothing remained human.

Photograph by Edward S. Curtis, 1914

Field Museum of
Natural History, Chicago

Tall figures of animals and legendary beings were carved from cedar trees and set up outdoors as totems. This mythical grizzly bear was made by the Bella Coola of British Columbia. It was displayed by the Indians at the World's Columbian Exposition, a world's fair held in Chicago in 1893, where thousands of people saw Northwest Coast Indian art for the first time.

The wooden figure at right, more than twenty feet high, has arms outstretched to grab little children. It represents a Tsonokwa, or Cannibal Woman, an evil creature in Kwakiutl mythology who steals food and furs from families. She also gathers children in her basket and takes them to her home deep in the forest where she cooks and eats them.

A story is told of a boy whose family fished for salmon, then hung them over fires to dry out so there would be food for the winter. The fish disappeared and the boy went to look for them. He found the salmon in the home of a Tsonokwa who had stolen the fish along with great quantities of other food. The boy recovered the food, killed the Tsonokwa and captured her children. Then he took her name to use in ceremonial dances and placed four carved images of the creature outside his house.

Photograph by
Edward S. Curtis,
1914

Tlingit,
Denver Art Museum,
photograph by Alfred Tamarin

On the Northwest Coast, food was easily available from the seas, the rivers and the dense forests, so there was no need for the Indians to plant crops. The only thing they grew was a little tobacco. In the summer women gathered shellfish, seaweed and berries, as well as edible leaves, mosses, ferns, bulbs and roots, birds' eggs and fruits. The stone pestle at left was for daily use, to grind food on a flat surface.

During the long winter there was time for visiting, and great feasts were held to display one's wealth and share surplus food. Guests often came from long distances by canoe and stayed for days. At these feasts the most handsome ceremonial garments were worn and enormous quantities of food were served.

Tlingit,
National Museum of Natural History,
Smithsonian Institution

Kwakiutl,
M. H. de Young Memorial Museum,
San Francisco

The wooden frog, hollowed out and painted with clan symbols, and the horned animal, holding a human figure in its paws, are small feast dishes.

At the feasts, dried fish was dipped into candlefish oil. For serving the oil, ladles carved of mountain sheep horn were used. Mountain sheep horn was acquired by trade with Indians of inland areas. The horn, which is curled, was boiled until soft, then straightened to a gentle curve. The rough form of the ladle was cut and it was put into a wooden mold to cool and harden into shape. Final carving was done afterward.

Tlingit,
Portland Art Museum

The winter months were also a time for religious ceremonies. Beautiful masks and costumes turned people into various characters bound up with clan traditions. The Kwakiutl ceremonials, especially their dances held to initiate youths into secret societies, were the most dramatic. Masked figures darted about, appearing and disappearing. Some Kwakiutl masks were eight to ten feet long.

In the photograph below, Kwakiutl dancers are participating in a winter ceremony. Some are wearing huge articulated, or movable, masks representing mythical cannibal birds. By pulling a string, the wearer could cause the lower beak to flap open and shut, or the entire mask to open, revealing a human face.

Photograph by Edward S. Curtis, 1915, Library of Congress

The Brooklyn Museum, photograph by Alfred Tamarin

Museum of the American Indian, Heye Foundation

Strips of red cedar bark are attached to the rims of the masks. Other clan members, in masks, ceremonial costumes and forehead helmets, stand by. At far left is the chief. He is holding a speaker's staff and wearing a neck ring of cedar bark, the symbol of the winter ceremony.

The mask above left, in the form of a bird, opens to reveal a double-headed serpent and other figures painted on the inside of the bird's beak. The inner mask is a dramatic face of a man. The outer face of the mask on the right is surrounded by mythical fish. When the strings are pulled, the mask will open and an inner face will be revealed.

Denver Art Museum,
photograph by Alfred Tamarin

Bukwus, the Wild Man of the Woods who appears in Kwakiutl tribal dances, lives in the forest in an invisible house and eats ghost food. He jumps about in uncontrolled frenzy, whooping or blowing through a small whistle hidden in his mouth. The face mask at left was made for Wild Man of the Woods dances.

The Tlingit mask at right, which belonged to a shaman, or medicine man, represents a legend about an old woman who may have practiced black magic. A frog emerges from her mouth and land otters cling to her cheeks. Spirits, land otters and frogs are lined up over her forehead, probably to indicate that these evil spirits, which drive people mad, possess her.

Her eyebrows and nose are made of copper and her eyes are inlaid with buttons. The Indians got the buttons from Russian traders who collected the skins of fur seals, sea otters and other fur-bearing animals to sell in Russian and Chinese markets. Chinese coins brought back to America by traders were also used for eyes on Indian masks.

Museum of the American Indian,
Heye Foundation

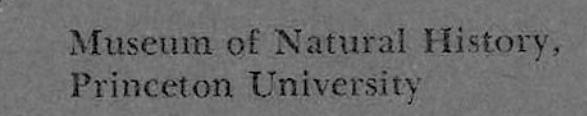

Museum of Natural History,
Princeton University

The realistic Haida mask of a woman at left has rawhide straps attached to the sides to hold it in place during dances. Designs are painted on the mask. Facial painting and tattooing with totems of a clan was practiced by both men and women. Arms, backs of hands, legs and bodies were also tattooed.

The face at right, above, which may be a likeness of a real person, is thought to represent one of the female spirits who dwell in the sky, the clouds and glaciers. She is wearing a labret, or lip plug. Large labrets were a sign of wealth and high social rank. As part of a ceremony when she came of age, a young girl would have a small slit made just below her lower lip. As the years passed, larger and larger labrets would be inserted into the slit.

The Tsimshian carved beautiful portrait masks which were used by secret societies and by shamans. This mask of a girl has decorations painted on her forehead and cheeks. Tied to her braids are ornaments of mythical bird figures that open and close.

Tlingit,
Peabody Museum,
Harvard University

Portland Art Museum

Photograph by Edward S. Curtis, 1914

When European explorers arrived on the Northwest Coast, they saw Indians in dugout canoes that were sometimes longer than their own sailing ships. The canoes in which the Indians went to war could be more than sixty feet long and eight feet wide, able to carry as many as fifty men more than five hundred miles on the ocean.

Ceremonial visits were made in canoes, painted with crests of the owner, that held about a dozen people. At left a group of Kwakiutl Indians in canoes are celebrating a wedding. After they had seen European sailing ships, the Indians began to make sails out of cedar bark mats, as shown in the photograph below.

To make a canoe, a cedar tree was carefully chosen and chopped down. When the wood dried, the general shape of the boat was carved out. Then, to soften the log, it was partly filled with water, which was heated by dropping in hot stones. The canoe was covered with wet mats to steam the wood until the sides could be stretched. When the wood dried, it was smoothed both inside and out.

Photograph by Edward S. Curtis, 1914

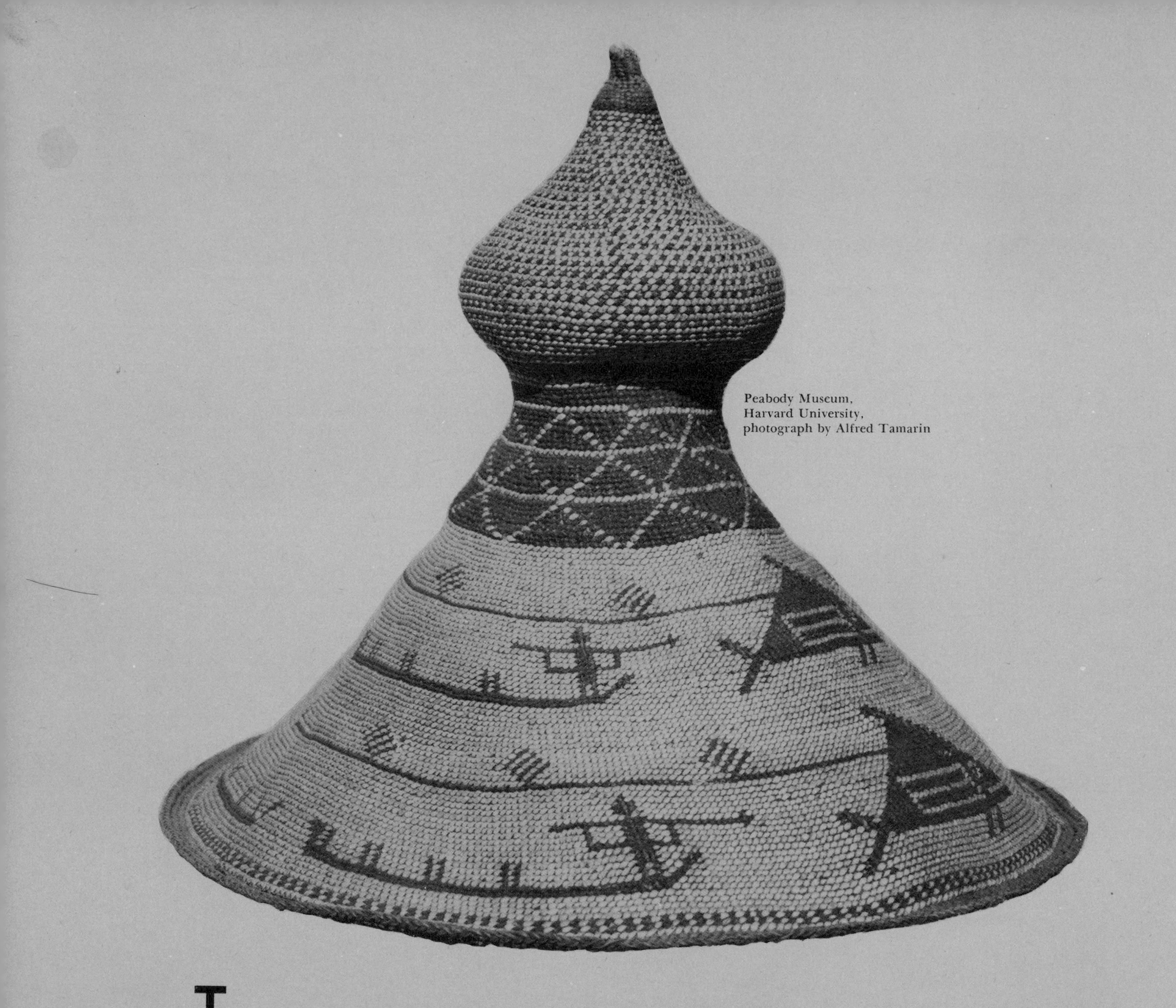

Peabody Museum,
Harvard University,
photograph by Alfred Tamarin

The most seaworthy canoes were made by the Nootka, who were famous for their whaling skill. Harpooning a whale from a bobbing boat on the open sea was extremely difficult and was thought to require magic power. Before starting on an expedition, a Nootka chief would pray, and the crew would fast. At sea, when a whale was sighted, the chief always had the honor of being the first to thrust in his harpoon. Sealskins filled with air were attached to the line on the harpoon to keep the dead whale afloat until it was dragged to shore. Afterward, a great feast would be held for everyone in the village. Whale flesh and whale blubber were used for food and were also traded.

Fred Harvey Fine Arts Collection,
The Heard Museum, Phoenix, Arizona,
photograph by Alfred Tamarin

A scene of a whale hunt decorates the Nootka hat at left. Bark from the cedar tree was woven in two layers, with the design of bear grass on the outer layer. Woven hats were light and comfortable and good protection from both rain and sun. This hat was collected by Meriwether Lewis and William Clark, who reached the Northwest Coast on their explorations of the West in 1805.

A design of a killer whale decorates the Tlingit basket above, made from roots of the spruce tree. The design is woven of bear grass and other native materials. In early times colors for the dyes used in baskets were made from mosses, roots, berries and tree bark. After the arrival of white settlers, factory dyes were used. Tlingit women were known for their fine weaving. Some of their baskets were so closely woven they could hold water.

Museum of the American Indian, Heye Foundation

Tlingit women also wove hats that were painted with clan designs. The cedar bark hat above is painted with clan symbols representing the raven. Both this hat and the one on the carved wooden figure at left have four potlatch rings. A potlatch is a great feast at which gifts are distributed. Each time a man gave a potlatch he would add another ring to his hat.

At right, a woman at a potlatch wears a cedar bark blanket and a hat decorated with abalone shell. Her nose ring and earrings are also made of abalone, which was imported by trade with Indians of California.

The inner bark from cedar trees was used to make clothing, as well as mats, sails, rugs, mattresses and cushions. To prepare it for weaving, strips of bark were shredded on the edge of an old paddle or soaked in sea water, then pounded with a whalebone tool to separate the fibers.

Lowie Museum of Anthropology, University of California, Berkeley

Kwakiutl,
photograph by
Edward S. Curtis,
1914

Tlingit,
Peabody Museum,
Salem, Massachusetts

Cedar bark was woven with wool from the wild mountain goat into splendid blankets known as Chilkat blankets. Northwest Coast Indians had no domestic animals except for a few small dogs raised for their woolly hair by the Coast Salish. Women wove the blankets on a simple loom. The designs were painted on boards by men, then copied by women. It took about six months to weave one blanket.

Chilkat blankets, which display family crests, are usually black, blue-green, yellow and grayish white. The white is the natural color of the mountain goat wool. The dye for the black was made from charcoal or graphite, the blue-green from copper salts and the yellow from a lichen, or fungus.

The blankets have always been considered valuable. They were sold and traded, worn at ceremonies by chiefs and noblemen, and used as burial robes by many Northwest Coast Indian tribes.

At left is a view of a Chilkat blanket spread out so that its entire design can be seen. Geometric forms fill in all the spaces between the clan designs. At right a Kwakiutl woman, dressed for a dance, wears a Chilkat blanket, a wooden mask and a cedar bark neck ring. When she danced, the fringe at the bottom of the blanket swayed to and fro.

Photograph by Edward S. Curtis, 1914

Tlingit, National Museum of Natural History, Smithsonian Institution

Chilkat blanket designs were also woven into long shirts. The climate is usually mild in the Northwest Coast. Before white settlers changed the ways of the Indians, men wore no clothes at all except for ceremonies or in bad weather. In good weather women wore only cedar bark skirts. Everyone went barefoot.

When traders brought factory-made blankets to the Northwest, the Indians began to decorate them by cutting figures out of cloth and sewing them onto the blankets, then outlining the figures with sea shells. With only simple tools, it was difficult for the Indians to cut the shells and drill holes in them. When pearl buttons were introduced by traders, they took the place of the shells. The body of a bear, its features and even

Tsimshian, University Museum, University of Pennsylvania

its internal organs were sewn on the blanket above and outlined with buttons.

Button blankets were highly valued and were worn by both men and women at ceremonies. They were popular as potlatch gifts and on the death of a chief might be placed on his grave.

Portland Art Museum

This wood carving of Owl-Man, decorated with a ribbon, was placed on a table at feasts honoring the memory of a Tlingit man who had been killed when a tree fell on him. His body was discovered when crows gathered around it. The figure of Owl-Man is said to have been carved from the fallen tree. It has an owl's body and a man's head with human hair. Owl-Man sits on a crow.

Almost all Northwest Coast Indian art was made and displayed to prove that the owner was descended from noble ancestors and that he had connections with the supernatural, but the charming little bear at right may have been carved just for amusement or for trade. Three-dimensional figures are usually carved more realistically than figures carved or painted on a flat background.

On the surface of the bear, blade marks from an adze, a curved tool used in wood carving, can be seen. Early carvers used stone, horn or shell tools, or beaver teeth set in wooden handles. The first iron was probably washed ashore from shipwrecked European or Asian vessels. Later, iron tools brought by traders made it much easier to carve large objects.

This figure of a man, carved of wood and painted, is standing on an animal head that represents a totem of the Tlingit. The man wears a wolf head helmet.

Lowie Museum
of Anthropology,
University of
California, Berkeley

Haida or Tlingit,
Lowie Museum of Anthropology,
University of California, Berkeley

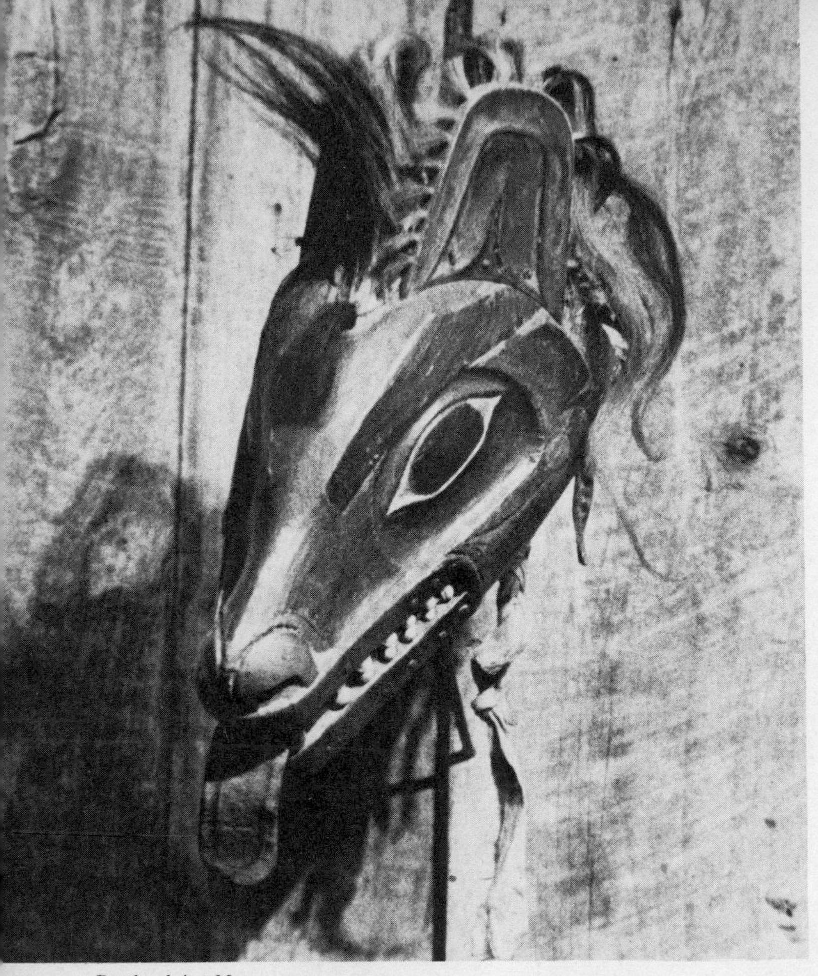

Portland Art Museum,
photograph by Alfred Tamarin

A member of a Tlingit clan that claimed the wolf as a totem wore the helmet at left, known as the hungry wolf, for ceremonial dances. The man would dance to a special clan song that was considered to belong to the hat. The wolf head has a long leather tongue and real animal teeth and hair. Its mouth and nostrils are made of copper, a metal that was considered highly valuable. The original owner

University Museum,
University of Pennsylvania,
photograph by Alfred Tamarin

of the helmet exchanged
four slaves for this copper.
Before wearing the helmet,
the dancer would polish
the copper brightly, singing
a special song.

Sometimes war helmets became ceremonial hats. The one at left, carved with the heads of a raven and a frog, belonged to a chief of the Chilkat, a group of the Tlingit. When he wore it, the chief's face would be painted with crest designs. Facial painting was done either freehand or with wood block stamps.

The hollowed bodies of a winged frog and a killer whale made graceful shapes for helmets worn in ceremonial dances by Tsimshian Indians.

National Museums of Canada

National Museums of Canada

National Museum of Natural History,
Smithsonian Institution

The painted wooden hat above has a bear on top of it to identify the clan of the Haida owner. The eyes of the bear are made of copper. A human figure is perched on the animal head of the Tsimshian hat at right. The little man wears a tall hat, with three rings that stand for the potlatches the owner had given.

At a potlatch guests are entertained, then presented with valuable gifts. In return each guest must have his own potlatch and try to give away even more valuable things. A potlatch might be held when someone changed his name, got married, became an adult, built a house or erected a totem pole. From the early 1900's until 1953, potlatches were forbidden by the Canadian government and discouraged by the American, but now they are again held in some villages.

Indians of the Northwest Coast, wealthy from the enormous supply of fish in local waters and from a thriving fur trade, distributed costly objects at these elaborate feasts in order to have high social standing. Social rank was considered extremely important. The chiefs and their wives were at the top of the social ladder. Artists were praised and had high status. Until slavery was outlawed, slaves were held in the lowest esteem.

National Museums of Canada

Slaves were obtained by trade or taken in warfare or in raids on neighboring villages. In battle, hide shirts were often worn over wooden armor. The shirt at left was made of two layers of buckskin, for double protection, joined together by strips of rawhide. A jumping killer whale and a human face are painted on the front. Hide shirts were also worn on ceremonial occasions.

Warriors wore wooden helmets carved with fierce human faces to frighten the enemy. They also wore broad collars made from straight pieces of wood which were softened by steam and bent into shape.

Armor breastplates to protect the body were made of slats of cedar wood fitted closely together. The slats were connected with cedar bark or spruce root twine and the breastplate was joined together with rawhide straps. All of this armor is Tlingit.

Ethnographical Department, Historical Museum, Berne

Helmet: Lowie Museum of Anthropology, University of California, Berkeley; collar: National Museum of Natural History, Smithsonian Institution

Peabody Museum, Harvard University

Nootka,
British Museum

Bows and arrows, clubs, spears and daggers were the main weapons for warfare. Wood and stone clubs were being used when Captain Cook landed on the Northwest Coast. This carved wooden war club, decorated with tufts of human hair, was collected by Cook and taken to England.

European seamen who came after Cook remarked in their journals that the Indians were experienced traders. They demanded a high price for their furs, rejecting trinkets and insisting on valuable metal, which they used for tools and weapons.

Metal fighting knives were considered symbols of power. The hilt, or handle, often represented an animal known for its bravery and fearless fighting. The double-edged copper dagger at right has strips of rawhide wrapped around the grip. The hilt ends in the shape of a bear's head, with mouth and eyebrows of copper,

Tlingit,
Peabody Museum,
Harvard University

eyes of shell, and hair of bear fur. This dagger would have been used in hand-to-hand combat.

Large flat sheets of copper in the shape of shields, usually more than two feet high, were prized objects. Much of the copper came from local soil but sometimes it was obtained in trade. "Coppers" were used as money and were often traded for blankets, which were the most important medium of exchange. Each time a copper was sold its price would rise. One once sold for twenty thousand blankets. Coppers were displayed at ceremonies, and sometimes at the end of a potlatch a wealthy man would break a copper to prove that he could afford to destroy valuable property. When this was done, others were expected to break their coppers too.

Tlingit, Museum of Primitive Art

Denver Art Museum,
photograph by Alfred Tamarin

The Haida make figures from carbonaceous shale, black rock which is found on the Queen Charlotte Islands in British Columbia and nowhere else in the world. The stone is soft when mined, so it is easily carved. Then it hardens after exposure to the air. The carvings take on a jet-black shine when polished by rubbing.

The figures are made for trade with visitors. The Haida began carving them in the early nineteenth century, after seeing the scrimshaw made by crew members of the whaling ships that came to the Northwest Coast. Scrimshaw are bone and ivory articles that whalers carved to occupy themselves on their long voyages.

The Haida chief at left is made of carbonaceous shale. He wears a blanket over his shoulders, a dance kilt, or skirt, decorated with totem designs and edged with a fringe, and a dance headdress with a crownlike ornament known as a frontlet. Headdresses with frontlets were worn on

National Museums of Canada

ceremonial occasions and at potlatches by men and women of noble birth.

Frontlets were carved with animals or birds illustrating an event in clan history or a legend of the tribe. The Tsimshian crest above represents a human surrounded by frogs. The teeth and eyes are made of abalone shell.

Haida,
National Museum
of Natural History,
Smithsonian Institution

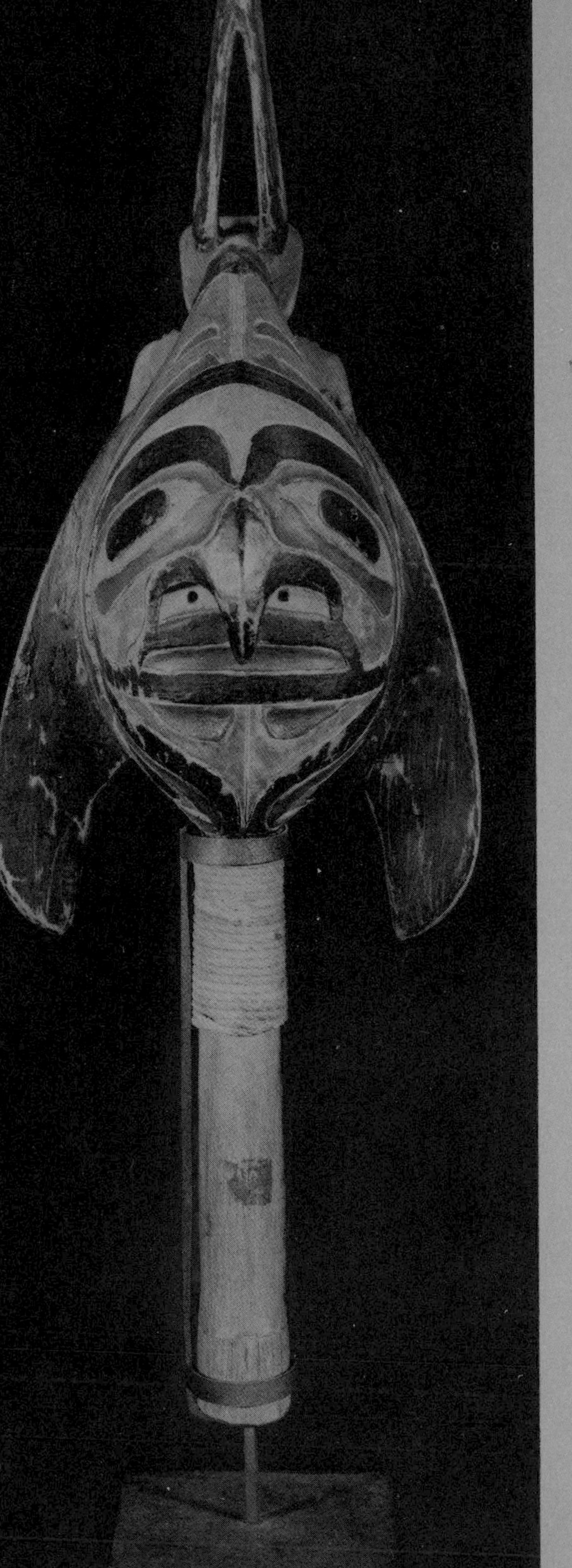

Haida, Arizona State Museum,
University of Arizona,
photograph by Helga Teiwes

Tlingit,
National Museum
of Natural History,
Smithsonian Institutio

Musical accompaniment was important to the ceremonies of chiefs and shamans, or medicine men, who shook rattles when they called on spirits. Even their dance skirts had puffin beaks, deer hoofs, animal teeth or claws sewn onto them to make sounds when they moved. As they danced and sang, they also beat skin drums and blew whistles to announce the coming of spirits. And rattles were used when an important speech was being made or when men went to war.

Wooden rattles were usually carved out of alder wood and filled with pebbles. They were made in many shapes. Human figures, animal heads and birds, especially ravens, were common. The rattle at far left is in the form of a raven with a masked medicine man reclining on its back. The shaman is holding a bird's tongue in his mouth to suck out poison, which was considered useful in casting spells and curing disease.

The underside of a bird-shaped rattle, center left, has a face representing a hawk, which perhaps stands for the sun. The rattle in the form of a man is decorated with hair and even has a mustache and beard.

Carved stick rattles called clappers, which make a loud noise when shaken, were made of pieces of wood, split and hollowed out, then wrapped together. This clapper forms a killer whale with an outstretched figure underneath.

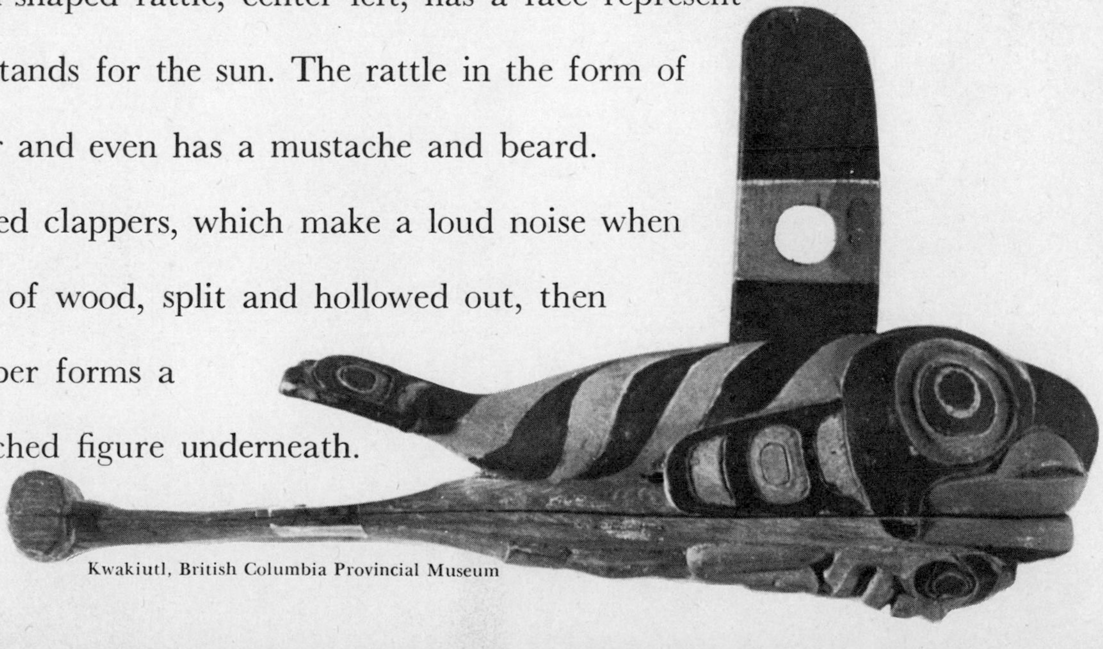

Kwakiutl, British Columbia Provincial Museum

Tsimshian, National Museums of Canada

Shamans were thought to have supernatural powers, which they received from spirits who appeared to them. Among their powers were controlling the weather, predicting the future, bringing success in war or the hunt, curing disease and finding those who were lost.

It was believed that if a person's soul strayed away, through illness or misfortune, he would soon die. A shaman would try to capture and hold a soul that had strayed with a soul catcher, a hollow bone object that was worn on a necklace or sewn to the shaman's dance cape or apron. The one above has an open-mouthed mythical animal at each end.

Tiny bone or ivory charms representing spirits were also worn by the shaman. Sometimes he touched them to the body of the patient whom he was trying to cure. The ivory figure of a woman in a tall hat, holding a child, is carved from a whale's

Haida,
Peabody Museum,
Salem

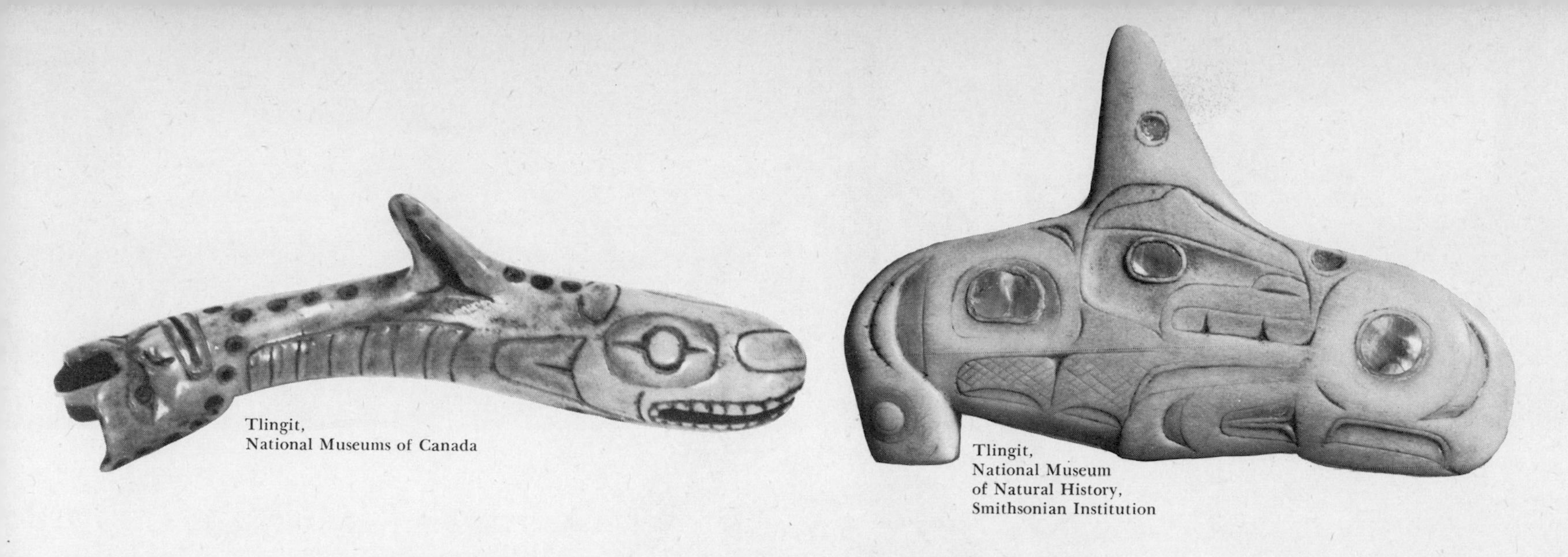
Tlingit,
National Museums of Canada

Tlingit,
National Museum
of Natural History,
Smithsonian Institution

tooth. The killer whale above left, with a spirit face on its tail, is made from a walrus tusk. The bone charm above right, also in the shape of a killer whale, is inlaid with shell. Charms were sometimes made from bear's fangs.

Antler was used for the spirit canoe in the shape of a sea lion, below. The seven figures represent people who were drowned when their boat was seized by an octopus. Among Salish groups, shamans performed a ceremony in which they paddled a spirit canoe to the land of the dead to bring back the soul of a person who had become ill because he had lost his soul.

Tlingit,
Museum of the American Indian,
Heye Foundation

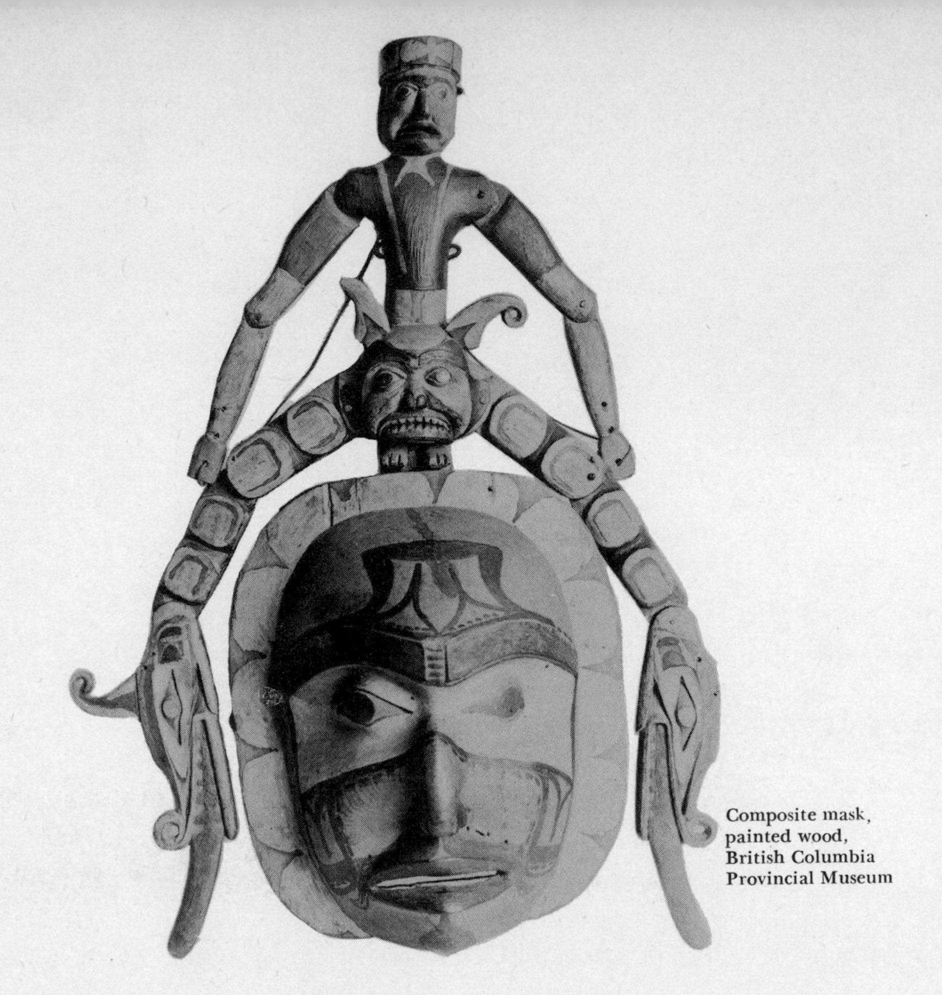

Composite mask,
painted wood,
British Columbia
Provincial Museum

Northwest Coast art arose out of the old culture of the Indians and was rooted in the old way of life. When that way of life changed, the art forms also changed, because the need for them was gone.

Yet some of the old practices persist. Some of the groups still give feasts in the ancient potlatch tradition. Craftsmen trained as carvers continue to teach their skills to younger men who understand their artistic heritage. And people of the Northwest Coast still show talent and skill in their boat building and woodworking. Today some of the art styles continue in new forms that combine the Indian tradition with modern art.